California Chinese Chatter

Also from Westphalia Press
westphaliapress.org

The Idea of the Digital University

Masonic Tombstones and Masonic Secrets

Eight Decades in Syria

Avant-Garde Politician

L'Enfant and the Freemasons

Baronial Bedrooms

Conflicts in Health Policy

Material History and Ritual Objects

Paddle Your Own Canoe

Opportunity and Horatio Alger

Careers in the Face of Challenge

Bookplates of the Kings

Collecting American Presidential Autographs

Misunderstood Children

Original Cables from the Pearl Harbor Attack

Social Satire and the Modern Novel

The Amenities of Book Collecting

The Genius of Freemasonry

A Definitive Commentary on Bookplates

James Martineau and Rebuilding Theology

No Bird Lacks Feathers

The Young Vigilantes

The Man Who Killed President Garfield

Anti-Masonry and the Murder of Morgan

Understanding Art

Homeopathy

Ancient Masonic Mysteries

Collecting Old Books

The Boy Chums Cruising in Florida Waters

The Thomas Starr King Dispute

Ivanhoe Masonic Quartettes

Lariats and Lassos

Mr. Garfield of Ohio

The Wisdom of Thomas Starr King

The French Foreign Legion

War in Syria

Naturism Comes to the United States

New Sources on Women and Freemasonry

Designing, Adapting, Strategizing in Online Education

Gunboat and Gun-runner

Meeting Minutes of Naval Lodge No. 4 F.A.A.M

California Chinese Chatter

by Albert Dressler

WESTPHALIA PRESS
An imprint of Policy Studies Organization

California Chinese Chatter
All Rights Reserved © 2014 by Policy Studies Organization

Westphalia Press
An imprint of Policy Studies Organization
1527 New Hampshire Ave., NW
Washington, D.C. 20036
info@ipsonet.org

ISBN-13: 978-1-63391-107-9
ISBN-10: 1633911071

Cover design by Taillefer Long at Illuminated Stories:
www.illuminatedstories.com

Daniel Gutierrez-Sandoval, Executive Director
PSO and Westphalia Press

Rahima Schwenkbeck, Director of Media and Marketing
PSO and Westphalia Press

Updated material and comments on this edition
can be found at the Westphalia Press website:
www.westphaliapress.org

加省華人之趣談

CALIFORNIA CHINESE CHATTER

SAN FRANCISCO
ALBERT DRESSLER
1927

"CALIFORNIA CHINESE CHATTER"
FOREWORD

To the reader the contents of this book may at times appear comical. It is not my purpose to lampoon, and I wish to state, here, my attitude toward the Chinese. I have high regard for the Celestial Brethren, and I am ready at all times to accord them the respect I consider due them, because of their achievements, and most ancient lineage.

> "The heat of the tropical sun shines down,
> What matter the skin be black or white;
> For white, or yellow, or black or brown
> Are equal, at last, in the Master's sight."

To those interested in the history of the State of California, and to those inclined toward the humorous, it is not amiss to call attention once again to the adage, "Truth is stranger than fiction." The truth herein contained is represented by 120 telegrams, exchanged among the Chinese, to and from Downieville, Sierra County, California, in the year 1874. It provides the reader with a heretofore unnoted aspect of California's Melting Pot. It offers a glimpse into the realism of her romance, as yet unknown save to a local few, and rising solely on its own merit it proclaims the atomic part of that Entity to which it belongs.

There is color abundant and diversified in these messages, as also in the most interesting transcript of the court proceedings in the trial of Ah Jake, a Chinaman who was tried for murder—dargow*—over a pair of boots. Throughout the book there appear new and unexpected stimuli. As one reads along toward the heart of the theme, due apology is offered to the dignity that may demur to the text and illustrations—if any.

—Albert Dressler.

*Dargow—Chinese word for fight.

CALIFORNIA STATE LIBRARY

SACRAMENTO

March 21 1927

Mr Albert Dressler

    2263 Geary Street

        San Francisco California

Dear Mr Dressler

      I have been greatly interested in the collection of old telegrams which were sent by Chinese in 1874, and which you have so generously given to the California State Library. They clearly form the basis for a series of "queer queue tales" of law suits, mine fights, kidnapped women and opium traffic sufficient for a place on the front page of a metropolitan daily, or a movie mystery thriller. The Downieville of the '70's was evidently not a sleepy little village. And who could imagine so many Chinamen in such a telegraphic hurry!

      I thank you for your kindness.

      Sincerely yours

          Milton J Ferguson
          State Librarian

CONTENTS

	Page
Telegrams by Chinese	1
Examination upon a charge of murder	41
Extracts from correspondence relative to Ah Jake	58
Ending	62

ILLUSTRATIONS

Frontispiece	IV
Fac-simile letter—Milton J. Ferguson	VIII
Drawing—Ah Quick	16
Fac-simile telegram—Fook Sing	18
Drawing—Traveling De Luxe in 1874	24
Fac-simile telegram—Ah Tri	26
Fac-simile telegram—Ah Jake	30
Drawing—Sam Wo Wash House, Sierra City	32
Drawing—Chinatown, Downieville	34
Fac-simile—San Francisco China News	40

CALIFORNIA CHINESE CHATTER

TELEGRAMS

EXCHANGED BY THE CHINESE TO AND FROM DOWNIEVILLE, SIERRA COUNTY, CALIFORNIA, DURING THE YEAR 1874.

Paradox though it seems, East and West have met at last in the following telegrams, as the East is represented by the California Chinese, and the West by the Western Union. The efforts of the Mongolian men to master the telegraph, back in 1874, revealed in "Pidgin" English, form an important sidelight on early life in the Golden West.

Sometimes we, who are accustomed to associate the Chinaman with laundries, Chop Suey and Joss Houses and as Vegetable Vendors, overlook the role played by this same Chinaman in the development of California. In the 'Seventies the Chinaman, his queue tucked into his hat, his shirt outside of his pantaloons, rubbed shoulders with the red-shirted miner, with the railroad builder, with the carpenter and with the merchant. The Chinaman of the 'Seventies wanted to be an American, hence he imitated the American's ways to the best of his ability.

In these telegrams such things as opium, slave girl traffic, money matters and mining claim troubles are treated with forceful candor. The messages being terse, mostly all "Quick," give an illuminating angle as yet untold, to the Rough and Ready Days.

Marysville, Cal.,
March 1, 1874, 10 A. M.

Quong Wo & Co

I no saby you, no can pay man, you send money I pay.
13 Collect 75c   Quong Hing Lung

———o———

Quong Chung Shing & Co   Downieville, Cal.,
724 Com'cl St., San Francisco   March 3, 1874.

Git Wo. I want you pay your cousin Ah Hoey expenses to come Downieville quick attend to claim. Am afraid there will be big fight. Answer.   Fong Sing
28 words Pd. $1.75   Kim Bayo

———o———

Hop Wo   Downieville, Cal.,
Care Kong You & Co   March 3, 1874
728 Com'cl St., San Francisco

Chinamen can't compromise about claim. Afraid they get fighting. Send man up quick today. Come today sure. Answer.   Tong Wo
20 words Pd.   Tie Yuen

———o———

San Francisco, Cal.,
March 3, 1874, 11:40 A. M.

Fong Sing

Ah Hoey not here. Hop Wo Company and Nin Yung Company send men tonight. You no feel bad.
18 Collect $1.25   Quong Chung Shing & Co.

TELEGRAMS

San Francisco, Cal.,
March 4, 1874, 3:30 P. M.

Fong Sing

Ah Hoey gone Virginia City. Two go up yesterday. Stop no fights.

12 Collect $1   Quong Chung Shing & Co

---o---

Downieville, Cal.,
March 4, 1874

Ah Chu
Stockton

Trouble about mining claims. I own' a share and all the company want you come. I want you come. Ans yes or no.

26 words Pd. $3   Fong Sing
Ah Jake

---o---

Stockton, Cal.,
March 4, 1874, 8:50 A. M.

Ah Jake

Partner gone San Francisco. I care business. No time come. Send letter, see what I do.

15 Collect   Ah Chee

---o---

Stockton, Cal.,
March 4, 1874, 7:04 P. M.

Ah Jake

Very busy have no got time. What is your lawsuit?

10 Collect $1.00   Ah Chee.

Stockton, Cal.,
March 5, 1874, 7:25 P. M.

Fong Sing

  I can't come now. Put your suit off. I try come soon.

14 Collect   Ah Chee.

---o---

Virginia, Nevada
March 5, 1874, 9 P. M.

Fong Sing & Kim Bayo

  I don't saby lawsuit for me to come. Send expense by telegraph. Answer.

14 Collect 75c   Ah Hoey

---o---

Downieville, Cal.,
March 6, 1874

Ah Chee
Stockton, Cal

  I will put the lawsuit off until next Monday. Will you come up sure. Answer quick.

16 Words Pd. $2.00   Ah Jake

---o---

Elko, Nevada
March 6, 1874, 9:20 A. M.

Ah Hug

  I have no got time.

5 Collect $1.00   Gee Lee.

Stockton, Cal.,
March 6, 1874, 10:30 A. M.
Ah Jake

My partner come back, come; if he no come back I can't come.

13 Collect $1.50   Ah Chee

———o———

Stockton, Cal.,
March 6, 1874, 12:07 P. M.
Ah Jake

Do not telegraph me no more. I come soon me can.

10 Collect $1.50   Ah Chee

———o———

Downieville, Cal.,
Hi Wo   March 7, 1874.
Marysville

Tell Six Company men to come quick. Fong Sing's lawsuit commences today. Answer quick tonight.

                                Ty Yuen & Co
                                Quong Wo & Co
23 words Pd. $1.25   Hong Wo & Co

———o———

Downieville, Cal.,
G G Clough   March 7, 1874.
Camptonville, care Jones

I would like to have you assist Vanclief in China case. No work. Fee fifty dollars. Answer.

17 words Pd. 45c   Ah Jake

Camptonville, Cal.,
March 7, 1874, 7:25 P. M.

Ah Jake

If no delay all right will be there tomorrow.
9 Pd.   G G Clough

———o———

Downieville, Cal.,
March 10, 1874

Yuen Lung
Stockton, Cal

Has Ah Chee started for Downieville. If not, tell him start right away. Answer
14 Pd. $1.50   Ah Jake

———o———

Stockton, Cal.
March 10, 1874, 5:15 P. M.

Ah Jake

Have your suit put off. My partner not come back yet. When he come I telegraph.
17 Collect $2.00   Ah Chee

———o———

Virginia, Nevada
March 12, 1874, 5:50 P. M.

Fong Sing

Ah Hoey go Virginia four days ago for Downieville. If he no come to Downieville send to San Francisco for him.
21 Collect $1.25   Sam Sing

TELEGRAMS

Downieville, Cal.,
March 12, 1874

Hop Sing
Camptonville

Did Ah Hoey get in your place tonight by stage. If so tell him to come right up quick. Answer.
20 words Pd. 50c   Fong Sing

———o———

Downieville, Cal.,
March 13, 1874

Gee Lee
Elko, Nevada

Tell Mow Sing to come Downieville. I in trouble have a big lawsuit on my hands. If he will come I will send him money to pay all of his expenses. Answer quick.
34 words Pd. $3.50   Fong Ahug

———o———

Elko, Nevada
March 13, 1864, 3:40 P. M.

Tong Ah Hing

He can't come got business to attend to.
8 Pd.   Gee Lee

———o———

Stockton, Cal.,
March 14, 1874

Ah Jake

Start tomorrow you want me come up. Answer quick.
9 Collect $1.00   Ah Chee

Sacramento, Cal.,
March 16, 1874, 2:50 P. M.

Fong Sing Store

Tell Ah Gek that Chu Chee will be Marysville today and Downieville tomorrow.

13 Collect   Chu Chee

---o---

North San Juan, Cal.,
March 21, 1874, 6:50 P. M.

Fong Wo

Why don't Yu Wo Ah Ching come back. When will be he here. Answer quick.

15 Pd 35c   Quong Tai Jan

---o---

San Francisco, Cal.,
March 25, 1874, 1:24 P. M.

Tai Yuen

Don't sell your opium.

4 Pd. 75c   Kong Yuen Chong

---o---

San Francisco, Cal.,
March 25, 1874, 2:25 P. M.

Fong Wo & Co
 Opium too dear
3 Pd   Yu Wo & Co

San Francisco, Cal.,
March 26, 1874, 10:10 A. M.

Quong Wo & Co

Opium up to one hundred and sixty dollars. Send down some money. We bought some before.

16 Collect   Quong Wo Lung

———o———

Downieville, Cal.,
March 27, 1874

Yen Mow
Nevada, Cal.

Case all settled. Expense so much have no money to send. Get money from some one else to go San Francisco.

20 words Pd $1.00   Quong Wo & Co

———o———

Downieville, Cal.,
March 28, 1874

Yu Wo & Co
717 Dupont St., San Francisco

What the price of opium. Answer.

6 words Pd. 75c   Fong Wo & Co

———o———

San Francisco, Cal.,
March 28, 1874, 4:05 P. M.

Fong Wo & Co

Now price hundred sixty dollars each hundred vials. Opium will be higher.

12 Pd.   Yu Wo & Co

Virginia, Nevada
March 29, 1874, 11:33 A. M.
Yuk Tong
 Yuk Tom you lie you jap boy gon Shanghi come or answer.
19 Pd $1.00   Luk Chung

———()———

Downieville, Cal.,
March 29, 1874
Luk Chung
Virginia, Nevada
 Yuk Tong all right. Don't understand what you mean. Answer.
10 words Collect   Yuk Tong

———o———

Virginia City, Nevada
March 30, 1874, 1:30 P. M.
Yuk Fong
 Did the girl Wah How no come here last month. I think she is kidnapped. Answer if she was.
19 Pd $1.00   Luk Chung

———o———

Downieville, Cal.,
March 30, 1874
Luk Chung
Virginia City
 She has not come here yet. Have never heard any one speak of her before. If I do I will telegraph.
21 words Collect   Yuk Fong

TELEGRAMS

Downieville, Cal.,
March 31, 1874

Won Lung
Stockton

    Case settled. Ah Chee went this morning on stage.
9 words Pd. $1.00   Ah Jake

———o———

Downieville, Cal.,
April 24, 1874

Cune Chong
Marysville

    Send one hundred and twenty dollars by telegraph to Fong Sing's Store. I send letter to you next mail. Trial on Monday. Answer.
23 Pd. $1.25   Lim Lung

———o———

Marysville, Cal.,
April 24, 1874, 6:25 P. M.

Fong Sing

    In few days will get men go up.
8 Pd 50c   Chung

———o———

Downieville, Cal.,
April 26, 1874

Cune Chung
Marysville

    Clough is sick. Get good lawyer. Send money quick. Trial tomorroy morning 10 o'clock. Case can't be postponed. Answer.
10 words Pd.   Fong Sing

Marysville, Cal.,
April 27, 1874
Received at Downieville 6:15 P. M.

Fong Sing

Hire a lawyer and if he wins case me will send one hundred and twenty dollars. If no win me send no money. The lawyer pay his own expenses. Answer immediately.

32 Pd. $1.75   Lem Chung

―――o―――

Alleghany, Cal.,
June 20, 1874, 7:40 A. M.

Tung Wo & Co. Store

Tell Lem Lun come over and cook for Miller. Bring two boxes opium. Answer.

14 Pd.   Ah How

―――o―――

Oroville, Cal.,
July 12, 1874, 9:55 A. M.

Fong Sing, Tie Yuen

Your woman she go Colusa. You want her go there.

10 Pd.   Lem Lun

―――o―――

Downieville, Cal.,
July 25, 1874

Kaw Chung
Wadsworth, Nevada

Don't you let her go. I will come over tomorrow and see her. I want to bring her to Downieville to live with me. What time does the train start. Answer quick.

32 words Pd.   Fook Sing

TELEGRAMS

Downieville, Cal.,
July 26, 1874

Wing Wo Chung
Wadsworth, Nevada

Fook Sing left today, will be in Wadsworth tomorrow. Tell her not to go to wait till he comes. Answer quick.
21 words Pd. $1.25   Tai Yuen

---o---

Downieville, Cal.,
July 26, 1874

Kaw Chung
Wadsworth

I will start for Wadsworth today and meet her on the way. Tell her to wait for me to come and if she wants to go I will let her. Don't care. Answer.
33 words Pd. $1.75   Fook Sing

---o---

Downieville, Cal.,
August 2, 1874

Hing Wah
Auburn

Ask Ah Tom if my partners Yuck Sing's woman down there. If you find where she stop answer immediately.
19 words Pd $1.00   Ah Tri

---o---

Downieville, Cal.,
August 2, 1874

Ah Tom
Auburn

Go and ask Mow Sing and he will tell you all about it and answer quick as you can.
19 words Pd. $1.00   Ah Tri

Auburn, Cal.,
August 2, 1874, 10:10 A. M.

Ah Tri

The woman is at Virginia. Come to Auburn and I will tell you heap lots.
15 words Pd.   Ah Tom

---o---

Auburn, Cal.,
August 2, 1874, 11:05 A. M.

Ah Tri

Woman went to Virginia town with How Ah Sing. You better come here and talk to the company. Keep quiet. I know all about it. It is all right.
28 Collect $1.50   Ah Tom

---o---

Nevada, Cal.,
August 3, 1874, 1 P. M.

Tie Yuen Company
Downieville

Gum Sing and woman arrested. Here tomorrow. Send sixty dollars.
10 words Pd.   Fook Sing

---o---

Nevada, Cal.,
August 4, 1874, 6:45 P. M.

Tie Yuen Co
Downieville

Man and woman in custody.
5 Pd.   E Barry

TELEGRAMS

Downieville, Cal.,
August 5, 1874

Fook Sing
Care Wing Wo Ching
Wadsworth, Nevada

Ah Tom write me Gan Que is at Auburn. You want catch her go right away. Answer.

17 words Pd. $1.00   Tie Yuen

———o———

Wadsworth, Nevada
August 6, 1874, 11:10 A. M.

Tie Yuen

I need two hundred dollars for expense. You send money to me and I will return it to you.

19 Pd.   Fook Sing

———o———

Downieville, Cal.,
August 6, 1874

Fook Sing
Wadsworth, Nevada

Come over here quick and I will see if I can let you have the money or not answer.

19 words Pd. $1.00   Tie Yuen

———o———

Nevada, Cal.,
August 7, 1874, 11:40 A. M.

I Yum

Barry, the woman and myself start for Downieville right away.

10 Collect Not charged   Fook Sing

Ah Quick says:
"He who writes must wait."

Sierra City, Cal.,
August 7, 1874, 9 P. M.
Ah Luk

No tend to go, You Dicks, he snatch my money last night. I take him back Sierra Valley tomorrow twelve o'clock. Answer I pay.
24 Pd.   Ah Sing

———o———

Auburn, Cal.,
August 12, 1874, 12:30 P. M.
Ting Yeu
Downieville

Fook Sing's woman has gone to Marysville.
7 Pd.   Ah Tom

———o———

Downieville, Cal.,
Len Tin   August 12, 1874
Oroville

Send me letter about woman quick.
6 words Pd.   Fook Sing

———o———

Downieville, Cal.,
Sing Lung, Ah Yik   August 13, 1874
Marysville

Bring woman up right away will pay three hundred dollars. Answer.
                                              Tie Yuen
13 words Pd. 75c   Fook Sing

The Western Union Telegraph Company.

ALL MESSAGES TAKEN BY THIS COMPANY SUBJECT TO THE FOLLOWING TERMS:

To guard against mistakes, the sender of a message should order it REPEATED; that is, telegraphed back to the originating office. For repeating, one half the regular rate is charged in addition. And it is agreed between the sender of the following message and this Company, that said Company shall not be liable for mistakes or delays in the transmission, or delivery, or for non-delivery of any UNREPEATED message beyond the amount received for sending the same; nor for mistakes or delays in the transmission or delivery, or for non-delivery of any REPEATED message beyond fifty times the sum received for sending this message, unless specially insured; nor in any case for delays arising from unavoidable interruptions in the working of their lines, or for errors in cipher or obscure messages. And this Company is hereby made the agent of the sender, without liability, to forward any message over the lines of any other Company, when necessary, to reach its destination.

Correctness in the transmission of messages to any point on the lines of this Company, can be INSURED by contract in writing, stating agreed amount of risk, and payment of premium thereon at the following rates, in addition to the usual charge for repeated messages, viz: one per cent. for any distance not exceeding 1000 miles, and two per cent. for any greater distance. No employee of the Company is authorized to vary the foregoing. The Company will not be liable for damages in any case where the claim is not presented in writing within sixty days after sending the message.

JAS. GAMBLE, Genl Supt., San Francisco.

WM. ORTON, President,
G. H. MUMFORD, Secretary, } New York.

Downieville Cal Aug 18 187 M.

Send the following Message, subject to the above terms, which are agreed to.

To Sing Lung Ah Yet Marysville

Bring her in a buggy
and I will meet you at
Camptonville come tomorrow
Fourthing

14 Words Pd 75

TELEGRAMS 19

Downieville, Cal.,
August 13, 1874

Sing Lung, Ah Yik
Marysville

Bring her in a buggy and I will meet you at Camptonville. Come tomorrow.
14 words Pd. 75c   Fook Sing

———o———

Downieville, Cal.,
August 13, 1874

Sing Lung, Ah Yik
Marysville

Watch woman close. I come tomorrow.
6 words Pd. 50c   Fook Sing

———o———

Downieville, Cal.,
August 13, 1874

Sing Lung, Ah Yik
Marysville

Is man who took woman there. Answer.
7 words Pd. 50c   Fook Sing

———o———

Downieville, Cal.,
August 13, 1874

Sing Lung, Ah Yik
Marysville

Will you bring man and woman. Answer.
7 words Pd. 50c   Fook Sing

Marysville, Cal.,
August 13, 1874, 8:15 A. M.

Fook Sing

Will you come by buggy or stage. I want to meet you outside of town. Answer immediately.

19 Collect $1.00   Sing Lung, Ah Yik

―――o―――

Marysville, Cal.,
August 13, 1874, 11:05 A. M.

Tie Yuen

Tell Fook Sing Min Que is here. What you going to do. Answer quick

16 Pd.   Sing Lung, Ah Yik

―――o―――

Marysville, Cal.,
August 13, 1874, 4:20 P. M.

Fook Sing

She wants you come right away and get warrant with officer, friends will help. You don't be afraid. We will get her sure.

23 Collect   Sing Lung

―――o―――

Marysville, Cal.,
August 13, 1874, 3 P. M.

Ah Sing Goon

Hom Game Sing take woman he stop here now. Fook Sing come quick to Marysville. Answer back.

17 Collect   Sing Lung, Ah Yik

TELEGRAMS

Marysville, Cal.,
August 13, 1874, 4:21 P. M.

Fook Sing
Care Eing Yue

Ask Fook Sing if he wants me to bring the woman back to his place. Expenses will be about three hundred dollars. If he is willing to pay it answer immediately. She might go off in a day or two.

42 Collect Sing Lung, Ah Yik

---o---

Marysville, Cal.,
August 14, 1874, 11:15 A. M.

Fook Sing

I want to know whether you come or not and what way you come. Answer.

15 Collect 75c Sing Lung

---o---

Downieville, Cal.,
August 14, 1874

Sing Lung
Marysville

Fook Sing go down stage this morning, be there tonight.

10 words Pd. 50c Tie Yuen

---o---

Marysville, Cal.,
August 15, 1874, 10:12 A. M.

Tie Yuen

I saw the woman but have not arrested her. Send marriage certificate.

12 Pd. Fook Sing

Downieville, Cal.,
August 15, 1874

Fook Sing
Marysville
　Will send the certificate next stage.
6 words Pd. 50c　　　　　　　　　　　　　　Tie Yuen

―――○―――

Truckee, Cal.,
August 26, 1874, 7:50 P. M.

Fong Sing
　I can't come tomorrow. Chinaman got killed, they want me to attend to him.
14 Pd.　　　　　　　　　　　　　　　　　　　Ah Jake

―――○―――

Downieville, Cal.,
October 4, 1874

Fook Sing & E Barry
Nevada, Cal.
　Is the woman in jail or not. If she is I will send money. Answer quick.
20 words Pd. 80c　　　　　　　　　　　　　Tie Yuen

―――○―――

Marysville, Cal.,
October 5, 1874, 9:20 A. M.

Eing Goon
　Send fifty dollars down by telegraph today to pay expense of woman go up to Nevada City. She name Gan Que. She come from Colusa today.
25 Collect　　　　　　　　　　　　　　　　Sing Lung

Marysville, Cal.,
October 5, 1874, 4:20 P. M.

Eing Goon

The woman is in jail here now. Send one hundred dollars today by telegraph for expenses to take the woman up to Nevada. You no send money she no go. Fook Sing he stop Nevada. You no got money, answer.

40 collect   Sing Lung

---o---

Downieville, Cal.,
Sing Lung   October 6, 1874
Marysville

I have not got any money here for Fook Sing. You pay all the expenses for the woman to go to Nevada and when Fook Sing comes up we will send it all back to you.

37 words Pd. $2.00   Tie Yuen

---o---

Marysville, Cal.,
October 6, 1874, 4:20 P. M.

Tie Yuen

Woman went up to Nevada this morning. I paid expenses one hundred twenty dollars. You send money tomorrow.

18 Collect   Sing Lung

---o---

Downieville, Cal.,
E Barry   October 6, 1874
Nevada

What do you think about this case. Have you got the woman or not. Answer immediately.

16 words Pd. 80c   Tie Yuen

Traveling Deluxe in 1874

TELEGRAMS

Nevada, Cal.,
October 6, 1874, 8:50 P. M.

Ah Tien, Ah Heing Store
  Send one hundred dollars, we have woman.

E Barry
7 words Pd   Fook Sing

———o———

Nevada, Cal.,
October 8, 1874, 10:45 A. M.

E Barry
  Kem Sing with officer go Downieville today. Hide woman. Answer.
10 Pd.   Ah Wan

———o———

Downieville, Cal.,
October 8, 1874

Ah Yu Dick
Sierra City
  Ah Chee send a dispatch to me saying that you snatch his money. Give it back to him and not make any trouble. Answer.
25 words Pd. 55c   Ah Tri

———o———

Marysville, Cal.,
October 9, 1874, 8:10 A. M.

Eing Goon, Fook Sing
  Last two time long pay fifty dollars, Colusa and policeman just now chinaman want money. Send it quick by telegraph.
22 Pd.   Sing Lung

THE WESTERN UNION TELEGRAPH COMPANY.

All Messages taken by this Company subject to the following terms:

To guard against mistakes, the sender of a message should order it REPEATED; that is, telegraphed back to the originating office. For repeating, one-half the regular rate is charged in addition. And it is agreed between the sender of the following message and this Company, that said Company shall not be liable for mistakes or delays in the transmission, or delivery, or for non-delivery of any UNREPEATED message beyond the amount required for sending the same; nor for mistakes or delays in the transmission or delivery, or for non-delivery of any REPEATED message beyond fifty times the sum received for sending this message, unless specially insured; nor in any case for delays arising from unavoidable interruptions in the working of their lines, or for errors in cipher or obscure messages. And this Company is hereby made the agent of the sender, without liability, to forward any message over the lines of any other Company, when necessary to reach its destination.

Correspondence in the transmission of messages to any point on the lines of this Company, can be INSURED by contract, in writing, stating agreed amount of risk, and payment of premium thereon at the following rates, in addition to the usual charge for repeated messages, viz: one per cent. for any distance not exceeding 1000 miles, and two per cent. for any greater distance. No employee of the Company is authorized to vary the foregoing. The Company will not be liable for damages in any case where the claim is not presented in writing within sixty days after sending the message.

W. M. ORTON, President.
O. H. MUMFORD, Secretary. } New York.

J. H. GAMBLE, General Sup't,
San Francisco.

Dated ____ Oct 7 ____ 1874.

Send the following Message subject to the above terms, which are agreed to.

To Ah Yu Dick Sierra City

Ah Chee sent a dispatch to me saying that you snatch his money give it all back to him and must not make any trouble answer

Ah Ine

25 ¼ 55 ft Words.

Sent at 7:45 a.m. by Q

TELEGRAMS

Marysville, Cal.,
October 9, 1874, 12:35 P. M.

Eing Goon, Fook Sing
Send fifty dollars here for tonight by telegraph hurry it quick. Answer.
14Pd.
Sing Lung

———()———

Downieville, Cal.,
October 9, 1874

Sing Lung
Marysville
What for you want fifty dollars.
6 words Pd. 50c
Fook Sing

———0———

Nevada, Cal.,
October 13, 1874, 1:30 P. M.

Tie Yuen
When you coming to pay. If not in few days will send officer after you.
15 Pd.
Hong Hi Wien

———0———

Nevada, Cal.,
October 15, 1874, 6:30 P. M.

Fook Sing, Care Tie Yuen
If you don't settle immediately will bring sheriff up. Answer.
10 Pd.
Hong Hi

Downieville, Cal.,
October 15, 1874

Hong Hi
Nevada
　Will send money down in two days.
7 words Pd. 40c　　　　　　　　　　　　Fook Sing

---o---

Marysville, Cal.,
October 24, 1874, 8:15 P. M.

Sing Goon
　Tell Fook Sing send money by telegraph come down Colusa policeman here now will wait till tomorrow money no come he go to Downieville to collect.
26 Collect　　　　　　　　　　　　　　Sing Lung

---o---

Wadsworth, Nevada
October 26, 1874, 10:15 A. M.

Fook Sing
　She will go down tonight if you want see her you will have to go to San Francisco.
17 Pd.　　　　　　　　　　　　　　　Kaw Chung

---o---

Jamison, Cal.,
October 28, 1874, 10:12 A. M.

Tie Yuen
　My woman sick, is she well or not. Answer telegraph.
10 Pd.　　　　　　　　　　　　　　　　Ah Jim

Downieville, Cal.,
October 28, 1874

Ah Jim
Jamison
    She all right now. Go Jamison few days.
8 Collect 25c   Tie Yuen

———o———

Downieville, Cal.,
November 2, 1874

Ah Jim
Jamison
    Your woman go to Sierra Valley be up tomorrow too much snow other way.
13 words Collect   Tie Yuen

———o———

Jamison, Cal.,
November 2, 1874, 4:30 P. M.

Tie Yuen
    I go to Sierra Valley today did my woman start.
9 Pd. 25c   Ah Jim

———o———

Downieville, Cal.,
November 2, 1874

Ah Jim
Jamison City
    Yes she started for Jamison this morning by eight o'clock on horse back she did not go by Sierra Valley.
20 words Collect   Tie Yuen

THE WESTERN UNION TELEGRAPH COMPANY.

All Messages taken by this Company subject to the following terms.

To guard against mistakes, the sender of a message should order it REPEATED; that is, telegraphed back to the originating office. For repeating, one-half the regular rate is charged in addition. And it is agreed between the sender of the following message and this Company, that said Company shall not be liable for mistakes or delays in the transmission, or delivery, or for non-delivery of any UNREPEATED message beyond the amount received for sending the same, unless specially insured; nor in any case for delays arising from unavoidable interruption in the working of their lines, or for errors in cipher or obscure messages. And this Company is hereby made the agent of the sender, without liability, to forward any message over the lines of any other Company, when necessary to reach its destination.

Corrections in the transmission of messages in any point on the lines of this Company, can be INSURED by contract in writing, stating agreed amount of risk and payment of premium thereon at the following rates, in addition to the usual charge for repeated messages, viz: one per cent. for any distance not exceeding 1000 miles and two per cent. for any greater distance. No employee of the Company is authorized to vary the foregoing. The Company will not be liable for damages in any case where the claim is not presented in writing within sixty days after sending the message.

WM. ORTON, President,
G. H. MUMFORD, Secretary, } New York.

JAS. GAMBLE, General Supt., } San Francisco.

Downieville Cal _Nov 16_ 1874.

M. _____

Send the following Message, subject to the above terms, which are agreed to.

To _Ah Wun Murada_

I cant do it I am going to leave
here for china tomorrow come up
yourself and get her

Ah Jake

Collier

19 Words. Sent at 5 P M., by ____

Nevada, Cal.,
November 6, 1874, 4:20 P. M.

I Yuen Store
   Gim Sing and Gan Que in jail send money quick.
10 Collect   Fook Sing

Nevada, Cal.,
November 6, 1874, 4:40 P. M.

Ah Tim, Ah Sing
   I take woman, good deal expense, send one hundred dollars by telegraph. All settled.
14 Collect   Fook Sing

Downieville, Cal.,
November 9, 1874

Sam Wo
Sierra City
   Woman Tie Ho come back today sure.
7 words Pd. 25c   Ah Oa

Nevada. Cal.,
November 16, 1874, 2:14 P. M.

Ah Jake, Fong Sing
   Can you bring Gan Que to San Juan right away. Answer.
10 Pd.   Ah Wein

Sam Wo Wash House
Sierra City, California

Downieville, Cal.,
November 16, 1874

Ah Wien
Nevada

I can't do it. I am going to leave here for China tomorrow. Come up yourself and get her.

19 words Collect   Ah Jake

———o———

Downieville, Cal.,
November 17, 1874

Sam Wo
Sierra City

Tell Fong Hing come tomorrow morning by seven o'clock. Answer.

10 words Pd. 25c   Hong Quong

———o———

Sierra City, Cal.,
November 17, 1874, 5:20 P. M.

Hong Quong

Send me right name who you want to come down. I don't know that name.

15 Collect 35c   Sam Wo

———o———

Downieville, Cal.,
November 17, 1874

Sam Wo Wash House
Sierra City

His name is Sam tell him to be sure and come down here by seven o'clock tomorrow morning. Answer he no come or not.

                                              John Sing
29 words Pd 65c   Tong Wo & Co

Yes, she is here.
Chinatown
Downieville, California

Downieville, Cal.,
November 19, 1874

Gan Que Yee Ah Sing
Nevada
    Gan Que go to Sierra City. Come up here quick. Answer quick.
11 words Pd. 60c   Ah Tim

———o———

Nevada, Cal.,
November 20, 1874, 8:04 A. M.

Ah Tim, Ah Mow
Care Jin Sing Store
    Will send officer up today to stop Gan Que. Answer.
10 Pd.   Ah Wein

———o———

Nevada, Cal.,
November 20, 1874, 4:30 P. M.

Wong Ah Yeu, Fong Sing Store
    Is Gan Que in Downieville. Answer quick.
7 Pd.   Ah Wein

———o———

Downieville, Cal.,
November 20, 1874

Ah Wein
Nevada
    Yes she is here.
4 words Collect   Wong Ah Yeu

Downieville, Cal.,
November 22, 1874

Quong Chung Shing & Co
724 Com'cl St., San Francisco
   Tell Ah Jake my brother came yesterday.
7 words Pd. 75c   Ah Hug

---o---

San Francisco, Cal.,
November 23, 1874, 2:45 P. M.

Tie Yuen
   You sent money to bank no check send check quick. Can't get money without check. Answer.
16 Pd.   Wee Ah Hong

---o---

Downieville, Cal.,
November 23, 1874

Kong Yuen & Co
San Francisco Calif
   The check is in letter that left here on the nineteenth last Thursday. You go to the bank and see if the check has been cashed or if it is lost. Give security for it and get the money. If the bank don't believe you have them telegraph to this bank.
57 words Pd. $3.00   Tie Yuen & Co

---o---

San Francisco, Cal.,
November 24, 1874, 8:30 A. M.

Fong Sing
   Send down the small account book to me.
8 Pd.   Ah Jake

TELEGRAMS

Downieville, Cal.,
November 24, 1874

Ah Jake
Care Quong Chung Sing & Co
724 Com'cl St., San Francisco

I did not get your message until this morning at nine o'clock. The stage had gone. Shall I take it to Camptonville and send it from there. Answer quick.
29 words Pd. $2.00   Fong Sing

———o———

San Francisco, Cal.,
November 25, 1874, 1:40 P. M.

Fong Sing
Send book tonight. I leave here next Tuesday.
8 Pd.   Ah Jake

———o———

Wadsworth, Nevada,
November 25, 1874, 2:30 P. M.

Eng Yuen, Fook Sing
Your woman go to San Francisco tonight with Lee Hung Sing Hoe go back to China you want to let her go answer quick.
23 Pd.   Kaw Chung

———o———

Downieville, Cal.,
November 25, 1874

Ah Jake
c/o Quong Chung Shing
724 Com'cl St., San Francisco

In this town everybody knows that Jim is gone back to China. Look out for him.
15 words, Pd. $1.00   Tong Hug.

Downieville, Cal.,
November 25, 1874

Quong Mow Lung
741 Com'cl St., San Francisco

Tell Ah Wing go Ah Lee collect money from Wo Tung He. Tung He comes from Downieville. Fong Sing's Ah Hug own brother.

23 words Pd. $1.50   Quong Wo

———o———

Downieville, Cal.,
November 27, 1874

Kong Yuen & Co
728 Com'cl St., San Francisco

Tell Ah Luk that Tong He will take the next steamer and go to China. Catch him and get the money if you can in any way.

27 words Pd. $1.75   Ah Tien

———o———

Downieville, Cal.,
November 27, 1874

Kong Yuen & Co.
728 Com'cl St., San Francisco

Tell Hom Chung that Wo Tong he owes my store one hundred and ten dollars. He is going to start for China very soon. Collect the money from him if you can.

32 words Pd $2.00   Tie Yuen

———o———

San Francisco, Cal.,
November 27, 1874, 8:45 A. M.

Fong Sing

Cowden is down there everything all right.

7 Pd.   Ah Jake

End of
Telegrams

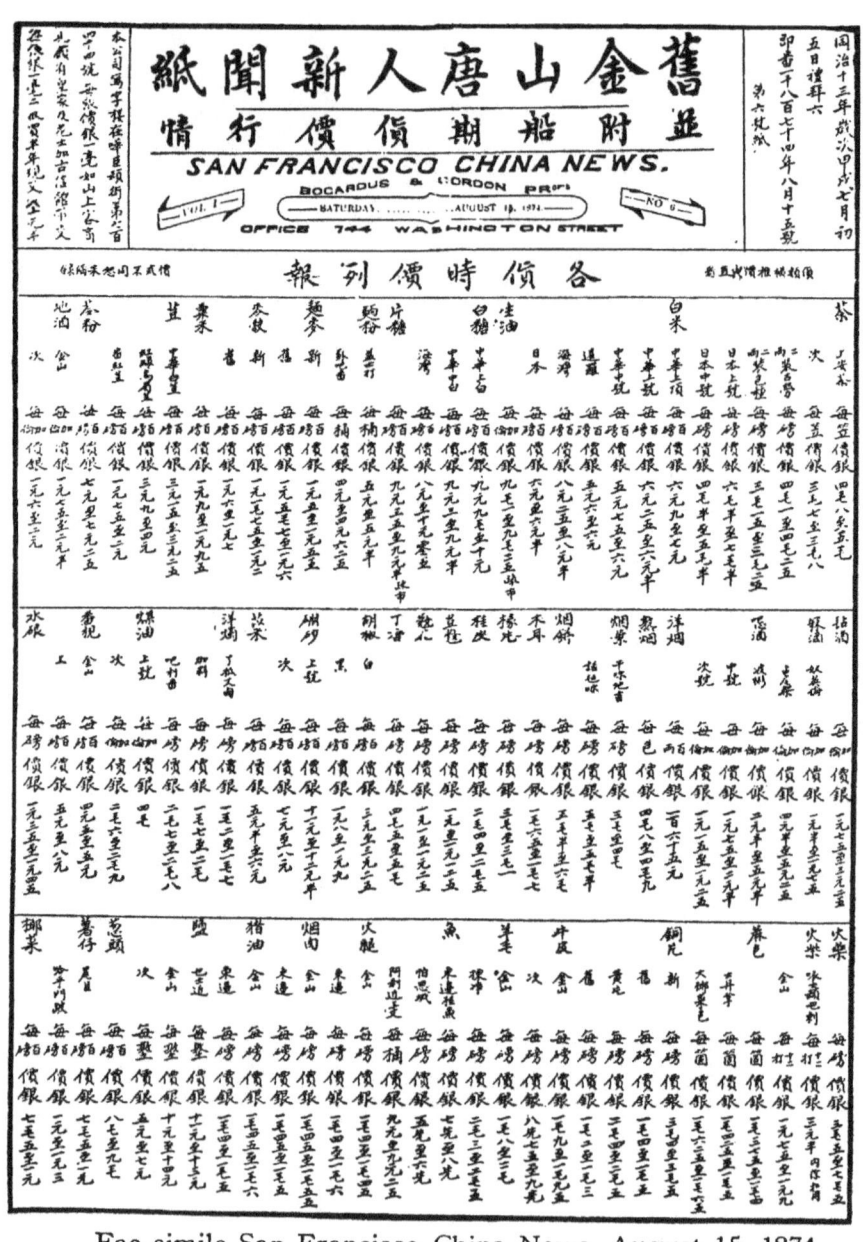

Fac-simile San Francisco China News, August 15, 1874

PEOPLE OF THE STATE OF CALIFORNIA

vs.

AH JAKE, Defendant.

———

EXAMINATION UPON A CHARGE OF MURDER

In the Superior Court of Sierra County, California.

Hon. F. D. Soward, acting as Magistrate.

Downieville, Sierra County,

October 23, 1874

Counsel Appearing:
For People: Dist. Att'y S. A. Smith.

Court. Case of the people of the State of Cal. vs. Ah Jake. An examination upon a charge of murder.

Under the provision of Section 869 of the Penal Code of this State, A. J. Meroux is appointed short hand reporter to take down the evidence and proceedings in the case.

(To Defendant.

Ah Jake, when you were brought before me yesterday evening, the information or complaint filed against you was read to you. At that time you stated you had no money with which to get an attorney. I will say to you now, however, that it is your right and privilege to have an attorney to represent you in every stage of the proceedings. Have you an attorney? Have you lawyer man?

Deft. I no got money.

Court. No money to get lawyer man?

Deft. No money; nother fellow take altogether——.

Court. Having no attorney I will say to you that it would be better for you not to say anything that will have a tendency to criminate you. The District Attorney will proceed with the case.

Mr. Smith. If your honor please, I would like to have this man Lo Kay sworn as interpreter.

Lo Kay sworn as interpreter.

AH TING.

Lo Kay, Interpreter. Sworn.
By Dist. Att'y Smith.

Q. State your name. Tell him to state his name.
A. Ah Ting.
Q. Place of residence; place of living. Where does he live?
A. Goodyears Bar.

EXAMINATION UPON A CHARGE OF MURDER 43

Q. Occupation or business? What business?
A. He keep garden. Grow vegetables. Gardner, he say.
Q. You know Wah Chuck in his life time?
A. He know him.
Q. When did you last see him alive?
A. Who? Which one?
Q. Wah Chuch.
A. Thursday.
Q. Who was with him at that time?
A. This man you mean. (Interpreter pointing at witness.)
Q. Wah Chuck.
A. With him. Wah Chuck with him.
Q. Where were you going?
A. Going down Downieville.
Q. To Downieville?
A. Yes.
Q. On what road?
A. He say that road going to Sierra City.
Q. Road between here and Sierra City?
A. Yes sir.
Q. Did you know the defendant, Ah Jake?
A. Yes.
Q. Did you meet him that day on that road?
A. He meet him on the road.
Q. What happened when you met Ah Jake the defendant?
A. He say buy pair boot. He ask Jake for pair boots; no give to him.
Q. Tell him to go right on and state what happened further.
A. He say he meet Ah Jake; he say he meet Ah Jake on the road and Wah Chuck he say Ah Jake steal his pair boot

and sack rice, he say. Then Wah Chuck he say he want tell Ah Jake——

(Defendant talks in Chinese to interpreter.)

Mr. Smith. I think the defendant interrupts the interpreter.

Court. Pay no attention to what he says. Just tell what the witness says.

A. He say he come down Wah Chuck; he meet in the road. Ah Jake use him pair boots. He ask Jake, he say give money send down to buy pair to him and make no more trouble. Jake say no, then Wah Chuck he want take off pair boots.

Q. Wanted him to take off the boots?

A. Yes, want him to take that off you know; then he take pistol and shoot him; take pistol out and shoot him; he take hand this way. Jake go after him he say.

Q. Witness run?

A. Yes.

(Defendant interrupts in Chinese.)

Interpreter. He say don't know what he say.

Court. You tell just what witness says that is all. Never mind what he say now.

A. He say Ah Jake shoot Wah Chuck and this man he see him shoot him; he fell down and he run! Ting he run. Ah Jake tell him come back; no run; tell him no run; you know what I mean tell.

Mr. Smith. Q. Tell witness no run?

A. Tell witness no go; he run.

Court. Q. Where be go then? What place this man go? You say he run. What place he go?

A. He run down this way; give one piece of paper to one family house; he run very quick; then he write one piece paper to Lew Barnhardt and tell him to come down to tell man;

give piece paper to Lew Barnhardt. He run Lew Barnhardt's house; you know that family house up the road; he don't know that house; that family house up there; he run right straight.

Court. Q. He saw Ah Jake shoot that man Wah Chuck?

A. Yes.

Mr. Smith. I guess we will have to lead him a great deal.

Q. When Ah Jake shoot Wah Chuck, what Wah Chuck do?

A. You mean Ah Jake shoot, what Wah Chuck do?

Q. Yes.

A. No say anything at all.

Q. What he do after he get shot? After he get shot what he do?

A. You mean Wah Chuck?

Q. Yes.

A. He say he fell down; no do nothing; no do anything.

Q. He bleed any? Did he go back after he went to Barnhardt's? Did he got back to where Wah Chuck was?

A. No.

Q. Did he see Wah Chuck afterwards? After he was shot?

A. He say he run down get buggy come up take him down.

Q. Did he see him dead afterwards?

A. He see him down here; no see him dead that place.

Q. Whereabouts he see him dead?

A. He say he see him Funk Kee store; outside door; take him down buggy; see him that time.

Defendant. He no see him dead; he lie.

Mr. Smith. Q. He saw him dead after that?

A. He don't know he dead that time or not; he say he shoot; that time he run.

Q. Did he see him afterwards in town here; see the dead body?

A. Yes, he see him.

Q. Was he dead then?

A. He was dead.

Q. When was that he saw him next, when he was dead?

A. Oh, he saw him many time; Fung Kee store first then China cellar.

Q. How soon after Ah Jake shot him did he see him dead? How long time after he shoot him he see him dead in town here?

A. He see Ah Jake shoot him; he don't know he dead that time or not; he don't know he dead; he don't know he dead or not up there.

Q. How long time was it he saw him in town?

A. He run down here; buggy pack him down; he find him dead down here Fung Kee store door; he find him here.

Q. How many hour?

A. He say he have no watch.

Q. It was on the same day that Ah Jake shoot him that he saw him dead, was it?

A. Yes, the same day.

Q. What Ah Jake shoot him with?

A. Pistol he say.

Mr. Smith. I don't know whether it is necessary to bring that pistol in here; it is loaded.

Court. I saw it last night.

Q. How far from town did the shooting take place? How far from this town?

A. He say he don't know; Chinaman call him little over two miles. He don't know; he no measure.

Q. That is probably about right. In what county? Sierra County, California?
A. That place there?
Q. Yes.
A. He say he don't know what county it is.
Q. What day? This was on Thursday last; last Thursday that the shooting took place.
A. Thursday he say.
Q. That is the 20th day of October, '87?
A. He say he don't know American what day is; he say it was Thursday.
Q. Last Thursday?
A. Yes. Last Thursday he say.
Q. Is this Ah Jake the man that did the shooting; that killed Wah Chuck? (Pointing to defendant.)
A. Yes.
The defendant in Court is pointed out by the witness as the one who shot Wah Chuck.
Court. To Defendant.
Q. You want to ask him some questions?
Defendant. Me askum him.
Court. You want to ask him some questions?
Defendant. He lie; he lie too much.
Court. You don't want to ask him any questions?
Defendant. Wah Chuck give him my money——
Court. You don't want to ask him any questions? You like to ask him some questions this man. You don't want to ask any question this man.
Mr. Smith. That is all I want to question this witness.
Defendant. He talk lie.

S. C. STEWART

Sworn.

Mr. Smith. Just state your name, residence and occupation, Mr. Stewart.

A. S. C. Stewart, residence: Downieville; sheriff of Sierra County.

Q. In what county is the roadway, highway between here and Sierra City?

A. Sierra County, California.

Q. Do you recognize the locality that the last witness described as the place where the defendant Ah Jake shot Wah Chuck?

A. As a matter of course I found the body lying on the side of the road.

Q. Whereabouts?

A. About I should say two miles and a half from Downieville; probably 300 yards above Lew Barnhardt's residence.

Q. The body of the Chinaman?

A. Body of the Chinaman called Wah Chuck.

Q. Dead or living?

A. Dead.

Q. What day was that?

A. Last Thursday.

Q. What day of the month?

A. 20th of October.

Q. 1887?

A. '87. 20th I believe; that is the way I figure it.

Q. The 20th of October, '87?

A. 1887.

Court. Last Thursday was the 20th.

Mr. Smith. Q. Did you examine the body, Mr. Stewart?

A. Partially. The body was lying on the side of the road

EXAMINATION UPON A CHARGE OF MURDER 49

lying on its face; feet drawn under him, and Mr. Myers came up. I didn't disturb him till he got there and we turned him over on his back.

Q. See any wounds on the body?
A. One wound in the left breast; near the nipple.
Q. Appeared to have been produced by what sort of an instrument or weapon?
A. Gunshot wound; pistol or gun; couldn't tell definitely which.
Q. Gunshot wound?
A. Yes sir.
Q. What time of the day was it you found the body?
A. I should judge in the neighborhood of one o'clock.
Q. In the afternoon?
A. Yes, in the afternoon.
Q. The place where you found the body was in what County and State?
A. Sierra County, State of California.

Mr. Smith. I guess that is all Your Honor; unless you desire to ask the witness or either of the witnesses some further questions.

Court. No it is merely preliminary, of course, and when it comes to trial he will have an attorney and bring out all the facts then.

Mr. Smith. I think there is cause shown for holding the defendant.

Court. (To defendant) Q. You want to ask Mr. Stewart some questions?
A. Yes sir.

Court. You ask him some questions if you want to.

Defendant. You see up here hole me fall? You see hole that stage road?

Mr. Stewart. I see two places.

Defendant. One place down river; one place down river; up road; two places; one place down river me fall down; you no see that time; you see up here two time?

Mr. Stewart. There were two places; two marks in the road——

Defendant. (Illustrating on floor)

He lay me down that way; he hold my queue that way; me tell him let me up; he no let me up. (Witness lays on floor making motion, etc., many of his remarks being unintelligible.)—Two time he come catch me; he come that side I catch that side— I no shootum him he shootum me; I tell him let me up.

Mr. Stewart. All I know about it there were two marks in the road there.

Defendant. One mark in the road one down side river; one mark down side; one mark up side— I catch him that side; he catch me that side. He shoot me I no know— I burn my coat— I no see him; he fight me back side; he catch my queue that way—he catch my queue; he make me scare— I no kill him, he kill me; he strong me. Four or five months ago I lend him $20.—He say three months ago he no give. He say he no give up here.—I say he give up here. He say G— d— you no got no money give you—G— d— s— b— you; he lay me down road; he strong me; I no can fight him; he big fellow; he stronger me; I no strong him; he make me fall four—three time—two or three time; he man more strong me; he fight me down.

Court. Do you want to ask Mr. Stewart any questions. You want to ask him some question. He don't understand what I say. Is that all?

Defendant. That all.

Court. You got any witness. You want some man swear?

Defendant. I no got man swear. Everybody help him. He talk lie. (Pointing to Ah Ting.) He talk lie; he no say take my queue; put on floor; he no talk; he no tell him— One hole down river that side— He talk lie; three time; he no hold my foot I no fall down at all; he hold my queue that way; first time he take my bag money; catch my money put him pocket; second time he catch my carpet sack; he say he kili me; I get scare; he catch me that side; I catch that side (Illustrating) I say I shoot you; I hold that way; shoot him that way; I think him scare; let go my queue, let me up; he lay me back side; me down side he up side; he no hold my foot I no fall down at all.

Court. (To Ah Ting)

Q. You see Wah Chuck touch Ah Jake; take hold Ah Jake?

Ah Ting. (Through interpreter) He say Ah Jake lie. Wah Chuck no touch him.

Court. Q. Wah Chuck no touch Ah Jake?

A. No.

Defendant. Talk him lie. He help Wah Chuck; no like me—that two men kill me; he like him; catch me.

Court. You say he take your money?

Defendant. A. He take my $30.

Court. One purse.

Defendant. That bag.

Court. He take your purse; he take your pocket book.

Defendant. I put one bag that side; I put down here, gold, gold coin.

Court. He take all your money?

Defendant. Two piece.

Court. Take two piece. He take all your money.

Defendant. One bag take him all; all two piece.

Court. How much money you have that other bag?
Defendant. I get thirty dollar
Court. How much you have other bag?
Defendant. That.
Court. Yes.
Defendant. I own that $4.65—60 cent; put little bag, carpet sack—that bag 65 cent; Four dollar; Four dollar sixty-five cent I keep that side; that side money I keep buy grub.
Court. What for you no have all your money in bag?
Defendant. That side buy grub that side buy boot.
Court. You no have all your money in your pocket book? Where you get that $30?
Defendant. I mine. Long time ago mining; one man give him change.
Court. Where you get that gold dust you have?
Defendant. Mining.
Court. What place?
Defendant. Two place; one Joss House; one man Goodyear Creek mining.
Court. One place Judge Howe?
Defendant. Joss House. One man up Goodyear Creek; my uncle.
Court. How long you have that gold dust?
Defendant. One month ago.
Court. What for you no sell him?
Defendant. I keep buy grub.
Court. I don't want to press him too strong as he has no attorney——
Q. How long you have that $30.
Defendant. I go house my partner tell me come up here come buy grub——
Court. He gave you the $30?

EXAMINATION UPON A CHARGE OF MURDER 53

Defendant. Yes.
Court. You put purse? You put your pocket book; you put in what pocket?
Defendant. That pocket.
Court. Gold.
Defendant. Gold coin.
Court. One twenty one ten?
Defendant. One twenty one ten, make $30.
Court. In the other pocket you keep silver.
Defendant. That pocket keep silver.
Court. This.
Defendant. Little carpet sack.
Court. What your partner name?
Defendant. Chung.
Court. What name?
Defendant. Chung.
Court. What place?
Defendant. Down Goodyear Bar.
Court. He down Goodyear Bar now?
Defendant. Mine down here.
Court. That Chinaman gave you $30?
Defendant. He mine, make him gold.
Court. He give you $30, buy grub.
Defendant. I come up here buy grub. Just now no mine now.
Court. What place you live?
Defendant. Down Joss House.
Mr. Stewart. Texas Bar.
Court. Texas Bar?
A. Yes.
Court. You want to say anything more. You wish to say anything more; you wish to talk any more?

Defendant. Little bit. He no rob my money I no shoot him. He rob my money; he say killum me; make me scare. Second time he catch my money he say killum me; I kill him first; he make me scare. I no kill him he kill me. I no kill him he kill me. He make me scare first. I think make him scare let me up; he say "You shoot me I no care G— d— s— b—." Make me scare I no want shoot him. I no know what place shoot him. I see last night my coat burn (Shows his coat with holes in it). I under him——

Court. What you say the man name who gave you the $30?

Defendant. Ah Chung.

Court. What pocket you have $30 in.

Defendant. This. (Showing left side.)

Court. You have the other this pocket.

Defendant. This pocket carpet sack.

Court. Little carpet sack this pocket.

Defendant. That side he catch first; second time he hold me that way I hold that way——

Court. Where you have your pistol? That time where you get your pistol?

Defendant. I put here; I put here. (Showing) My pistol that side——

Court. You have your pistol in here?

Defendant. Yes.

Court. Stuck in there.

Defendant. A. Yes; him that side; he hold me that way. He no hold my foot I no fall down.

Court. This man hold your foot. (Pointing at Ah Ting.)

Defendant. This man.

Court. This man here. (Pointing at Ah Ting.)

Defendant. He help Wah Chuck. He no help him I no fall down. He two men strong me. I one man; no strong enough fight him two men; he no hold my queue; no hold my foot I no fight him at all; he no rob my money I no shoot him; he say kill me; make me scare; I no kill him he kill me; other fellow hold my foot.

Court. This fellow here. (Pointing at Ah Ting)

Defendant. Yes. He lie. He no talk; he talk lie; he scare he no talkum.

Court. What company this man who was killed belong to? What company he belong to? Wah Chuck what company?

Defendant. All same place.

Court. Your Company?

Defendant. All same Hop Wo.

Court. He belong to same company?

Defendant. All same company.

Court. All belong to same one.

Interpreter. Six company— Hop Wo.

Court. All belong to the same company. You all belong to one company?

Interpreter. Six company all one; all same six company. One of six company——

Court. You say this man no like you ? (Pointing at Ah Ting.)

Defendant. He hold my foot.

Court. He no like you, this man?

Defendant. He no like me; he like him.

Court. You no like man killed either.

Defendant. He help Wah Chuck. He lie. He talk lie. He no talk hold my queue; he lie.

Court. You know this man long time?

Defendant. I see two year ago.

Court. You know man that was killed called Wah Chuck, long time?

Defendant. Know him long time ago.
Court. You have trouble before?
Defendant. No.
Court. Always good friend before?
Defendant. Always good friend before. No good friend no lend money; he no good friend I no lend money him at all.
Court. This man and you good friends all the time?
Defendant. Not much——
Court. You not good friends all the time?
Defendant. Not friends all the time.
Court. You enemy?
Defendant. Eh——
Court. He don't understand.
Interpreter. Sometime good sometime no good he say.
Court. He have trouble this man before.
Interpreter. He say maybe so, maybe not.
Court. Where you go after you shoot?
Defendant. I go down here.
Interpreter. He say he go down river.
Court. You go Forest City then?
Defendant. I shoot Wah Chuck I go down here— three Chinaman that house; I live that house; supper that night; Friday morning he give breakfast I go Forest City.
Court. You go Forest City? You try to shoot Henry Hartling when he take you?
Defendant. No.
Court. You know Henry Hartling man catch you Forest City; bring you over?
Defendant. (Through interpreter) He say come in catch him——
Court. You pulled your pistol? You took out your pistol?

EXAMINATION UPON A CHARGE OF MURDER

Defendant. (Through interpreter) He say no pistol—no shoot him.

Court. You no take out your pistol try to shoot him?

Defendant. No.

Interpreter. He say he no pack him that time.

Court. You got anything more you want to say; anything more?

Defendant. No.

Court. No witness?

Defendant. No.

Court. He will be bound over for the crime of murder without bonds.

Court. Where this man live? (Pointing at Ah Ting.)

Interpreter. Goodyear Bar.

Mr. Smith. I think it would be a good idea, Judge, to put this man under bonds to come to the trial as he might go away.

Court. Order will be made requiring him to give bail in the sum of $500 with two good and sufficient sureties to be approved by the Court. In case he fails to do that then he shall be confined in the County Jail abiding the further order of the Court. Sheriff will take charge of the defendant and take charge of the witness until he gives the bond that is required, to be approved by the Court.

———o———

I hereby certify that the foregoing is a correct transcript from my shorthand notes of the testimony of the witness given at the trial of the above entitled case, before Hon. F. D. Soward, Presiding Magistrate, Oct. 23d, '87.

A. J. MEROUX,
Reporter.

Downieville, Oct. 26th, '87.

EXTRACTS FROM CORRESPONDENCE RELATIVE TO AH JAKE

State Prison at Folsom
April 11, 1927

"In reply to your letter of the 10th instant in which you ask for certain information regarding Ah Jake, an early inmate of this institution, beg to advise that this prisoner was received at Folsom on November 28, 1888, under sentence of life on a charge of Murder in the First Degree.

"Ah Jake was first sentenced to death, the execution to take place in Sierra County, but Governor R. W. Waterman commuted the sentence to life on November 14, 1888, whereupon Ah Jake was transferred to Folsom Prison to serve his sentence

"Our records further show that on March 1, 1890, Ah Jake was transferred to San Quentin Prison. He remained there until November 18, 1891, when he was transferred to the Insane Asylum. Further than this our records do not go. Any other information you may need in connection with this case could probably be obtained from San Quentin Prison."

COURT SMITH, Warden

State Prison at San Quentin
April 15, 1927

"Ah Jake, No. 13998, received at San Quentin from Folsom Prison March 1, 1890, crime murder first degree, committed in Sierra County, sentence life—commuted from death sentence, pardoned January 1, 1891. When received here he gave his age as 40, nativity China, occupation cook. We have no record of his transfer to one of the asylums."

FRANK J. SMITH, Warden

EXTRACTS FROM CORRESPONDENCE

Stockton State Hospital
April 20, 1927

"We have examined our records and find the commitment of Ah Jake, dated Nov. 7, 1891, from Folsom Prison, and he was admitted on Nov. 9, 1891. The commitment shows that he had been held in Folsom Prison on account of the crime of murder. He was a native of China of the age of 35 at the time of commitment. Our records also show that he died on April 21, 1908, of Thombus, contributory Valvular Heart Disease, and his remains were buried in grave 3137 in the cemetery connected with this hospital."

FRED P. CLARK, Med. Supt.
By Geo. A. Brown, Jr., Sec'y,

Napa State Hospital
April 28, 1927

"Referring to your inquiry of April 19, regarding the Chinaman of the name of Ah Jake, this will inform you that I have personally gone over our register of male patients for a good many years back and am unable to find the admission of a Chinaman of that name during the early nineties. It frequently happens, however, that in the case of Chinese the names are turned around and twisted so that it is impossible to identify them. It is possible that the Chinaman was here under some other name."

G. W. OGDEN, M. D.,
Medical Superintendent
By R. E. Jeppey, Secretary

Yreka, California
April 28, 1927

"I find from our record that on February 19, 1890, one Ah Jake, convicted of murdering one Ah How, was sentenced to 13 years in Folsom Prison. Murder committed September 4, 1889. We have no record showing his commitment to asylum."

W. J. NEILON, County Clerk

Downieville Calif
April 29 1927

"Ah Jake killed Wah Chuck on the 20th day of October, 1887; was tried and convicted of murder in the first degree and sentenced to be hung, but he got a new trial and was sentenced to State Prison for life. He was later pardoned by the Governor. He is still living on Goodyear Creek. He is the same Ah Jake that was injured when you were here. He was pinned under a large rock for two days before he was discovered. He never was in any insane asylum to my knowledge.

. . . JOHN T MASON*

*NOTE: John Thomas Mason arrived in Sierra County, California, in 1851.

Downieville Calif
May 4 1927

"I wish to say that Ah Jake who was tried for murder over a pair of boots is still living and I know him very well. He is at Goodyear Creek about three miles from the little town of Goodyear Bar. I saw Ah Jake about three weeks ago and he is real well. He comes to Downieville about once a month and I buy gold from him."

. . . ANTONE LAVEZZOLA*

*NOTE: Antone Lavezzola is owner of the famous old St. Charles Hotel, Downieville, California.

ENDING

The preceding letters may seem puzzling to the reader. They have been presented here with the purpose of affording the public an opportunity to judge for itself concerning the ultimate fate of the Ah Jake of our story. It was found impossible to interview the Ah Jake living today at Goodyear Creek due to the fact that he had been seriously injured and was in a part of Sierra County inaccessible at the time I was investigating there, because of the heavy snows.

As there were two Ah Jakes sentenced to prison at about the same time, I am convinced that this is the Chinaman that dargowed with Wah Chuck over a pair of boots in our history. Although the people interviewed know little of his past, Ah Jake is well liked by those who know him today. At the time of Ah Jake's trial there was quite an amount of conspiracy existing among the Chinese, so it is probably that which accounts for the justice of his living through his serious adversities, leading a charmed life. As Bacon wrote, "Adversity is not without comforts and hopes."

The Editor.

An edition of 525 copies, twenty-five of which are reserved for private distribution, edited, illustrated and published by Albert Dressler, June First, Nineteen Twenty-seven, of which this is

Number *8 Gift Copy*
a. D.

San Francisco,
2263 Geary Street.

www.ingramcontent.com/pod-product-compliance
Lightning Source LLC
Chambersburg PA
CBHW022124040426
42450CB00006B/830